GNU LibreJS Reference Manual

A catalogue record for this book is available from the Hong Kong Public Libraries.

Published in Hong Kong by Samurai Media Limited.

Email: info@samuraimedia.org

ISBN 978-988-8381-61-6

Table of Contents

LibreJS

This manual is for GNU LibreJS (version 6.0.10, 25 October 2015).

1 Overview

GNU LibreJS —an add-on for GNU IceCat and Mozilla Firefox— detects and blocks nonfree nontrivial JavaScript while allowing its execution on pages containing code that is either trivial and/or free.

Many websites run nontrivial JavaScript on your computer. Some use it for complex tasks; many use it gratuitously for minor jobs that could be done easily with plain HTML. Sometimes this JavaScript code is malicious. Either way, the JavaScript code is often nonfree. For explanation of the issue, see "The JavaScript Trap"(http://www.gnu.org/philosophy/javascript-trap.html).

If you care about freedom in your computing, and don't wish to let all and sundry make you run nonfree programs, now you can prevent it by using LibreJS.

2 Disclaimer

- LibreJS is not a security tool. Its goal is to detect nonfree nontrivial JavaScript, and it currently does not detect whether free or trivial code is malicious or not. Other free Mozilla extensions and add-ons may be available for this purpose.

- LibreJS is always a work in progress. If you find a bug, please report it to `bug-librejs@gnu.org`.

3 Installation

You can install LibreJS directly using a generated `librejs.xpi` file, or by building it from source.

3.1 Building the Package

After installing `jpm`, you should be able to use the `make` command to build LibreJS from source.

After running `make`, a new file, `librejs.xpi` should be generated. This is the file that can be installed in a Mozilla browser.

3.2 Installing LibreJS

To install the add-on for all users, run:

```
sudo make install
```

or as root:

```
make install
```

Next time you open a Mozilla-browser as a user of your system, you should be notified that a new add-on (in this case, LibreJS) as been installed and whether to allow it to run or not.

4 How to Use

4.1 LibreJS in action

After installing the add-on, you will see the LibreJS widget in the add-on bar at the bottom of the browser window. After loading a page, left-click on the widget to view the deactivated JavaScript code from the page (both on page and external) and, if applicable, the scripts that were accepted.

4.2 Complaint Feature

It is very important to complain when a site has nonfree JavaScript code, especially if it won't work without that code. LibreJS makes it easy to complain by heuristically finding where to send the complaint.

When nonfree/nontrivial code is detected in a page, LibreJS attempts to find a relevant contact link or email for the website you are visiting. In order to do so, it will attempt to visit a few links from the current page (for instance, a link labeled "contact" on the same domain as the current page, ...)

LibreJS detects contact pages, email addresses that are likely to be owned by the maintainer of the site, Twitter and identi.ca links, and phone numbers.

After LibreJS detects any of the above, a "Complain" tab will appear on the right of your web browser. When you click on this tab, a large panel will appear with contact information. Ideally, at the top you will find the email address of the maintainer, labeled as the "Email you should use".

When you complain to the website for their nonfree nontrivial JavaScript, provide them with the link to the JavaScript Trap essay so that they can get more information on what the issue is and how they can solve it on their own site.

LibreJS includes a default subject line and body for the complaint email, with a link to the JavaScript Trap essay. This can be configured in the LibreJS add-on preferences in your web browser.

4.3 Options

Whitelist   LibreJS lets you whitelist domain names and subdomains to bypass the regular JavaScript check. This might be useful, for example, if you are running your own code in a local web server. In order to add a whitelisted domain or url, go to Tools >> Add-ons, or press *Control* + *Shift* + *A*. Inside the add-on window, click on *Extensions*, and in the list, where you see LibreJS, click on the *Preferences* button. You will see an input field labeled *Whitelist*. In the field, enter comma-separated domain names. Do not enter the protocol. For instance to whitelist all the pages of `http://www.gnu.org` and `https://gnu.org`, enter '**gnu.org**'. To allow all subdomains from gnu.org, enter: '***.gnu.org**'. This will match such sites as `http://savannah.gnu.org` and `http://audio-video.gnu.org`.

Complaint tab
> This specifies whether the complaint tab appears when a site is running nonfree JavaScript.

Display notifications of JavaScript analysis
> This option enables an info bar of realtime JavaScript analysis.

Complaint email subject
> Configure the default subject used in complaint emails.

Complaint email body
> Configure the default body used in complaint emails.

5 JavaScript Detection

LibreJS considers JavaScript on a page nontrivial if any of the following are true:
- It makes an AJAX request or is loaded along with scripts that make an AJAX request,
- It loads external scripts dynamically or is loaded along with scripts that do,
- It defines functions or methods and either loads an external script (from HTML) or is loaded as one,
- It uses dynamic JavaScript constructs that are difficult to analyze without interpreting the program or is loaded along with scripts that use such constructs. These constructs are:
  - Using the eval function
  - Calling methods with the square bracket notation
  - Using any other construct than a string literal with certain methods (`Obj.write`, `Obj.createElement`, ...).

In practice, the JavaScript code in your page may be found trivial by LibreJS if, as a whole:
- It does not define functions and it does not load external scripts (with the HTML src attribute in a `<script>` tag).
- It does not make AJAX calls.
- It does not load external scripts with dynamic constructs.
- It does not use constructs that may be used to do any of the above in a non-obvious way (use of the `eval()` method, use of square bracket method calls, use of concatenation with certain constructs or method calls, ...).

However, in some instances, you may be required by LibreJS to add a stylized comment to JavaScript code that may be otherwise trivial.

When an external file defines a function, it becomes available to all other external scripts. That is the case if another script defines a function that makes AJAX calls, when an external script loads other scripts dynamically (which in turn could also make AJAX calls, ...), or when a script is written with constructs that may do any of these.

For instance, if your page contains the following:

```
<script src="jquery.js"></script>
<script>
$.doSomething();
</script>
```

While `$.doSomething();` may seem trivial, you will nevertheless have to add a stylized license comment on your main HTML page because the external script (in this case jQuery) has been found to define methods that make AJAX calls. `$.doSomething()` might make an AJAX call, and LibreJS does not check for that. The rule of thumb is that when you use a library or code that handles AJAX, JSON, JSONP, the loading of scripts dynamically, you should have license mentions for all your JavaScript files and for your main page regardless. In practice this is a case that happens very often with code that uses libraries.

In practice also, the JavaScript code in an external file (an external `.js` file loaded on your page) may be found trivial if it does not define functions/methods.

And in the same manner it will be considered nontrivial if AJAX calls, dynamic script loading, or non-obvious dynamic JavaScript constructs are used in another script.

If your JavaScript code makes AJAX requests, it's important to get an accurate *Content-Type* in the response from the server. For example, if you're using JSON, set it to `application/json`. This is because LibreJS alters the content of `text/html` responses.

6 Free Licenses Detection

6.1 Detected Free Licenses

In order for a file to be detected as free, the license notice should appear in a JavaScript file above all code, at the very top of the file.

For inline JavaScript code inside `<script>` tags in HTML pages, the license notice should appear once per page as a comment inside a `<script>` tag, before all the code in that script. When the only inline JavaScript code is within element attributes (`onload`, `onclick`), place the license notice in an otherwise empty `<script>` at the top of the page. This is sometimes needed when an external script performs AJAX calls or embeds scripts dynamically, and the only inline JavaScript is an event attribute making a method call, e.g.:
`<body onload="methodCall('remote-data.xml');">`

When people speak of the "MIT license" they mean either the X11 license or the Expat license. Please see which license the code uses, and label it accordingly.

Currently LibreJS checks for the following licenses:

- Apache License, Version 2.0
  - Identifier: 'Apache-2.0'
  - URL: http://www.apache.org/licenses/LICENSE-2.0
  - Magnet link: 'magnet:?xt=urn:btih:8e4f440f4c65981c5bf93c76d35135ba5064d8b7&dn=apache-2.0.txt'
- Artistic License 2.0
  - URL: http://www.perlfoundation.org/artistic_license_2_0
  - Magnet link: 'magnet:?xt=urn:btih:54fd2283f9dbdf29466d2df1a98bf8f65cafe314&dn=artistic-2.0.txt'
- Boost Software License
  - URL: http://www.boost.org/LICENSE_1_0.txt
  - Magnet link: 'magnet:?xt=urn:btih:89a97c535628232f2f3888c2b7b8ffd4c078cec0&dn=Boost-1.0.txt'
- BSD 3-Clause License
  - URL: http://opensource.org/licenses/BSD-3-Clause
  - Magnet link: 'magnet:?xt=urn:btih:c80d50af7d3db9be66a4d0a86db0286e4fd33292&dn=bsd-3-clause.txt'
- CPAL 1.0
  - Identifier: 'CPAL-1.0'
  - URL: http://opensource.org/licenses/cpal_1.0
  - Magnet link: 'magnet:?xt=urn:btih:84143bc45939fc8fa42921d619a95462c2031c5c&dn=cpal-1.0.txt'
- Creative Commons CC0 1.0 Universal
  - Identifier: 'CC0-1.0'
  - URL: http://creativecommons.org/publicdomain/zero/1.0/legalcode
  - Magnet link: 'magnet:?xt=urn:btih:90dc5c0be029de84e523b9b3922520e79e0e6f08&dn=cc0.txt'
- Eclipse Public License 1.0
  - Identifier: 'EPL-1.0'
  - URL: http://www.eclipse.org/legal/epl-v10.html

- Magnet link: 'magnet:?xt=urn:btih:4c6a2ad0018cd461e9b0fc44e1b340d2c1828b22&dn=epl-1.0.txt'
- Expat License (sometimes called the MIT license)
  - Identifier: 'Expat'
  - URL: http://www.jclark.com/xml/copying.txt
  - Magnet link: 'magnet:?xt=urn:btih:d3d9a9a6595521f9666a5e94cc830dab83b65699&dn=expat.txt'
- FreeBSD License
  - URL: http://www.freebsd.org/copyright/freebsd-license.html
  - Magnet link: 'magnet:?xt=urn:btih:87f119ba0b429ba17a44b4bffcab33165ebdacc0&dn=freebsd.txt'
- GNU General Public License (GPL) version 2
  - Identifier: 'GPL-2.0'
  - URL: http://www.gnu.org/licenses/gpl-2.0.html
  - Magnet link: 'magnet:?xt=urn:btih:cf05388f2679ee054f2beb29a391d25f4e673ac3&dn=gpl-2.0.txt'
- GNU General Public License (GPL) version 3
  - Identifier: 'GPL-3.0'
  - URL: http://www.gnu.org/licenses/gpl-3.0.html
  - Magnet link: 'magnet:?xt=urn:btih:1f739d935676111cfff4b4693e3816e664797050&dn=gpl-3.0.txt'
- GNU Lesser General Public License, version 2.1
  - Identifier: 'LGPL-2.1'
  - URL: http://www.gnu.org/licenses/lgpl-2.1.html
  - Magnet link: 'magnet:?xt=urn:btih:5de60da917303dbfad4f93fb1b985ced5a89eac2&dn=lgpl-2.1.txt'
- GNU Lesser General Public License, version 3
  - Identifier: 'LGPL-3.0'
  - URL: http://www.gnu.org/licenses/lgpl-3.0.html
  - Magnet link: 'magnet:?xt=urn:btih:0ef1b8170b3b615170ff270def6427c317705f85&dn=lgpl-3.0.txt'
- GNU Affero General Public License, version 3
  - Identifier: 'AGPL-3.0'
  - URL: http://www.gnu.org/licenses/agpl-3.0.html
  - Magnet link: 'magnet:?xt=urn:btih:0b31508aeb0634b347b8270c7bee4d411b5d4109&dn=agpl-3.0.txt'
- The ISC License
  - URL: https://www.isc.org/downloads/software-support-policy/isc-license/
  - Magnet link: 'magnet:?xt=urn:btih:b8999bbaf509c08d127678643c515b9ab0836bae&dn=ISC.txt'
- Mozilla Public License 2.0
  - Identifier: 'MPL-2.0'
  - URL: http://www.mozilla.org/MPL/2.0
  - Magnet link: 'magnet:?xt=urn:btih:3877d6d54b3accd4bc32f8a48bf32ebc0901502a&dn=mpl-2.0.txt'
- Public Domain
  - Public domain is not a license (see https://www.gnu.org/licenses/license-list.html#PublicDomain). If you want to release your work to the public domain, the FSF recommends using CC0.

- Magnet Link: 'magnet:?xt=urn:btih:e95b018ef3580986a04669f1b5879592219e2a7a&dn=public-domain.txt'
- Universal Permissive License
  - Identifier: 'UPL-1.0'
  - URL: https://oss.oracle.com/licenses/upl/
  - Magnet link: 'magnet:?xt=urn:btih:478974f4d41c3fa84c4befba25f283527fad107d&dn=upl-1.0.txt'
- WTFPL
  - Identifier: 'WTFPL'
  - URL: http://www.wtfpl.net/txt/copying/
  - Magnet link: 'magnet:?xt=urn:btih:723febf9f6185544f57f0660a41489c7d6b4931b&dn=wtfpl.txt'
- X11 License
  - URL: http://www.xfree86.org/3.3.6/COPYRIGHT2.html#3
  - Magnet link: 'magnet:?xt=urn:btih:5305d91886084f776adcf57509a648432709a7c7&dn=x11.txt'
- XFree86 License
  - Identifier: 'Modified-BSD'
  - URLs: http://www.xfree86.org/3.3.6/COPYRIGHT2.html#3 http://www.xfree86.org/current/LICENSE4.html
  - Magnet link: 'magnet:?xt=urn:btih:12f2ec9e8de2a3b0002a33d518d6010cc8ab2ae9&dn=xfree86.txt'

6.2 Undetected Free Licenses

If you are using a free license that isn't detected by LibreJS and isn't listed in the previous section, please send a message to bug-librejs@gnu.org regarding this license, where code released under this license can be found, and where to find the license text and information.

Many free licenses are listed in this page: http://www.gnu.org/licenses/license-list.html

7 Setting Your JavaScript Free

The first step is releasing your JavaScript under a free license. If you are already using a free library, or you're not using any third-party libraries, it might only take a few minutes.

All JavaScript code on a web page (inline, on-page, and external) shares a common scope. Thus, code is generally either rejected or accepted as a whole by LibreJS. If some JavaScript code is found to be nontrivial and nonfree, then most of the time, all the the rest is discarded as well.

On your website, take a look at your HTML source. You can identify distinct pieces of JavaScript that might be free and some other that are nonfree.

Tip: By running LibreJS on your page, you will get a list of all the JavaScript that was blocked. This gives you an overview of the JavaScript in your page.

Imagine a page that contains several pieces of JavaScript from various sources:

- On top, within the `<head>` tag, it includes jQuery
- Then, some JavaScript code that you have written
- At the bottom, a JavaScript-based Facebook widget
- Also, there's some analytics tracking code

JavaScript that is already free

First, you must ensure that the library is free. If the file contains a copyright and a license notice, you won't need to look any further. But if there's no mention of the license, or if it's too brief, you'll have to look for a COPYING or LICENSE file within the original library's source package, or on the library's official website.

Your own JavaScript

The free license given to your code should be compatible with the rest of the JavaScript on a page. A good way to check is to read up on them: http:// www.gnu.org/licenses/license-list.html

Nonfree JavaScript

This might be the case with an analytics tracker, social media widgets, and code that runs ads. Removing these pieces of code from your site is required to have the rest accepted as free. There are often alternatives to nonfree libraries or to third-party services:

- If you have used nonfree third-party code as the base to write your own code, try to find a free alternative.
- If you're using a third-party service such as an analytics service, replace it with a free alternative like Piwik.
- If you can't find free JavaScript that has already been developed, write it yourself! Who knows, your own solution might be the start of a brilliant project!

7.1 JavaScript Web Labels

One way to make your website work with LibreJS is by defining a JavaScript Web Labels table.

A JavaScript Web Labels table is informative to both site visitors and the LibreJS program. You make a Web Labels table on a new HTML page that's linked to from your main page. The table lists each of your site's JavaScript files, that file's corresponding human-readable source file, and the canonical url of its free license.

When using a JavaScript Web Labels table for your own files, it's important to put a copying permission statement at the top of each source file listed in right-most column of the Web Labels table. For info on how properly release your code as free software, see `https://www.gnu.org/licenses/gpl-howto.html`. Future versions of LibreJS will require a copying permission statement or other license notice for source files listed in a Web Labels table.

More information on JavaScript Web Labels is detailed here: `https://www.gnu.org/software/librejs/free-your-javascript.html#step3` and here: `https://www.gnu.org/licenses/javascript-labels.html`.

7.1.1 Specifying multiple licenses for a single JavaScript file

If you compile or concatenate your JavaScript into a single file, the source files you're combining may be released under different licenses. You can specify multiple licenses for the file in a JavaScript Web Labels table, like this:

```
<table id="jslicense-labels1">
    <tr>
        <td><a href="all.min.js">all.min.js</a></td>
        <td>
            <a href="http://www.gnu.org/licenses/gpl-3.0.html"
                >GPL-3.0+</a>
            <br />
            <a href="http://www.apache.org/licenses/LICENSE-2.0"
                >Apache-2.0</a>
        </td>
        <td>
            <a href="gpl-script.js">gpl-script.js</a>
            <br />
            <a href="apache-script.js">apache-script.js</a>
        </td>
    </tr>
</table>
```

The `<br />` tags just make the table more understandable when looking at the rendered version of it on the license page. They aren't required by LibreJS.

If all the licenses contained in the second column are recognized by LibreJS to be free licenses, then LibreJS will allow the file in the first column to be run.

7.2 Adding a stylized comment in your JavaScript files and on your page

See a "Convention for releasing free JavaScript programs" in the JavaScript Trap `http://www.gnu.org/philosophy/javascript-trap.html`

Adding this notice will ensure LibreJS will find the JavaScript file to be free. The `@licstart` and `@licend` lines at the beginning and end of the stylized comment are necessary to make a clear statement that the _entire code_ in the file is free. This means that you must ensure that no nonfree code was carelessly appended at the end of the file.

In the main HTML page, the license notice covers JavaScript contained in all `<script>` tags with on-page code and the inline JavaScript (in event attributes such as onload, onclick, etc, ...). Since external files have their own stylized comment, they are not covered by the notice in the main HTML page. Make sure to identify all the licenses available. LibreJS will only ensure it matches a notice of an allowed license once, so the order does not matter, but the responsibility is on you to make sure all code is under the free licenses mentioned between `@licstart` and `@licend`.

You should make *only* one `@licstart` `@licend` comment in your page, since it pertains to the entire code on page across all `<script>` tags and inline html attributes.

When you use the JavaScript Web Labels method, you should still include a license notice at the top of each of your source files. This ensures that if someone copies the file and uses it for something else, the license remains intact.

For more info on making your JavaScript LibreJS-compliant, see this web page: `https://www.gnu.org/software/librejs/free-your-javascript.html`

8 LibreJS Development Notes

8.1 Running LibreJS from the source directory

Download `jpm`, then do something like this in the LibreJS directory:

```
jpm run -b `which abrowser`
```

8.2 Debugging

Uncomment lines 22 and 23 in `lib/main.js` to enable printing of `console.debug()` statements.

8.3 Adding new whitelisted libraries

Run the `data/script_libraries/gethash.sh` script, using the URL to a JavaScript file as the argument, then add the output of that command to `data/script_libraries/script-libraries.json`.

8.4 Releasing a new version

Update the version number in:

- `configure.ac`
- `package.json`
- `doc/version.texi`
- `data/display_panel/content/display-panel.html`
-

  Then run 'make info' to build the docs with `gendocs.sh`.
- 'git commit' and 'git tag 6.0.4'
- Export a tarball:
    - 'git archive --format=tar.gz --prefix=librejs-6.0.4/ 6.0.4
      >librejs-6.0.4.tar.gz'
    - 'mv librejs-6.0.4.tar.gz ~/releases/librejs-6.0.4/'
- Make xpi file: 'jpm xpi; mv librejs.xpi librejs-6.0.4.xpi'

Appendix A Installation Requirements

A.1 Mozilla Browser

You will need one of the many flavors of the Mozilla browser to use LibreJS. It can be installed on the following:

GNU IceCat, Mozilla Firefox, Trisquel Abrowser, Debian Iceweasel.

LibreJS works on these browsers starting from version 29. We recommend that you use the latest version of your Mozilla browser. LibreJS has been tested extensively on multiple GNU/Linux distributions, but it is compatible any operating system as long as you're using a compatible Mozilla browser.

A.2 Mozilla's Jetpack Manager for Node.js

LibreJS uses the Mozilla `jpm` tool, a set of utilities for creating, testing, running and packaging Mozilla Jetpack Addons.

You do not need `jpm` to use the LibreJS xpi file or to install it using the packaged version, but it is required in order to package the LibreJS source code into an xpi file. If you would like to run the tests for LibreJS or make changes to the source files, you will need `jpm` as well. For the "make" command to work properly, you must have the `jpm` command available on your system from the command line.

You can find information on getting `jpm` at these links:

`https://www.npmjs.com/package/jpm`

`https: / / developer . mozilla . org / en-US / Add-ons / SDK / Tutorials / Getting_Started_%28jpm%29`

JPM is released under the Mozilla Public License 2.0.

Appendix B LibreJS Internals

LibreJS intercepts HTTP responses and rewrites their contents after analyzing JavaScript within them. It does not remove script nodes and attributes from the page, but instead "deactivates" them by modifying the `type` and `src` attributes on script elements and by moving the contents of inline JavaScript attributes such as onClick into harmless attributes.

LibreJS detects the most common cases using the HTTP response method described above, but in extremely rare cases, or when running code locally, LibreJS cannot detect JavaScript during the response stage.

To remedy this issue, and as a final safeguard, LibreJS takes a look at the scripts that are about to be executed while the browser engine is parsing the page. If the script is not found in a list of accepted scripts populated earlier, the execution will be prevented. This is to ensure content types that are not regular HTML (binhex with HTML in it, ...) and JavaScript do not fall through the cracks and get executed.

Appendix C Tests

In order to better understand how LibreJS works, you can try to visit these pages with LibreJS installed and enabled and see how they are being processed:

- `http://lduros.net/assets/librejs/tests/trivial-inline-trivial-external/` This page contains trivial on-page JavaScript code, and an external script that contains trivial JavaScript code. Therefore, all JavaScript is being executed.

- `http://lduros.net/assets/librejs/tests/trivial-inline-nontrivial-external/` The on-page script here is trivial and uses a built-in method, but the external script in this page is nontrivial (defines a function.) The external script is blocked, the inline script is executed.

- `http://lduros.net/assets/librejs/tests/nontrivial-inline-trivial-external/` This page contains nontrivial code on page, and trivial code in its external page. All JavaScript is *removed* from the page, and the external script is never analyzed, since the nontrivial conditions are already met in the page.

- `http://lduros.net/assets/librejs/tests/free-inline-free-external/` This page contains free on-page (GPL 3) JavaScript, and free external Javascript. Therefore all JavaScript is being executed.

- `http://lduros.net/assets/librejs/tests/free-inline-nonfree-nontrivial-external/` This page contains free on-page JavaScript. The external script contains nonfree nontrivial JavaScript (AJAX request). The free code that is inline is executed, but the external file is blocked.

- `http://lduros.net/assets/librejs/tests/intrinsec-event/` This page contains trivial on-page code, with an intrinsic event in an html attribute (onload). All JavaScript is being executed.

- `http://lduros.net/assets/librejs/tests/trivial-inline-free-external-defines-function/` This page contains on-page trivial JavaScript (only makes a window alert and loads an external script using the html <script> tag with the src attribute. The external script is free (GPL v3), and since it is only nontrivial because it defines a function, the on-page trivial code is allowed to use it. All JavaScript is being executed.

- `http://lduros.net/assets/librejs/tests/trivial-inline-free-external-writes-script/` This page contains trivial on-page JavaScript code, and loads an external script that is free. Since no function is defined, the external script is being analyzed. The external script is free. Trivial here is not allowed because the external script, although free, writes a script. The inline trivial script should also have a free license notice for it to be interpreted.

- `http://lduros.net/assets/librejs/tests/shelltypist/demo/real-life-example-with-jquery-free.html` This is a real-life example of a small jQuery plugin. The on-page JavaScript code has a free license. The jQuery external file has a free licensed. The shelltypist.js file has a free license as well. All licenses are defined between `@licstart` and `@licend`. All JavaScript is executed.

- `http://lduros.net/assets/librejs/tests/shelltypist/demo/same-page-without-free-license.html` This is the same page than the previous example, except it does not have a free license for the main HTML page on-page script. While the actual code there is trivial, since jQuery defines methods that make use of AJAX, trivial code is not allowed, and no JavaScript is executed.

- `http://lduros.net/assets/librejs/tests/test-labels/` This page contains JavaScript (jQuery minified) that does not have proper license information in the file, as it has no `@licstart @licend` comment. It would be considered nonfree, however, the page itself uses the JavaScript Web Labels method. On the page itself, you will find a link labeled "JavaScript License Information", which leads to a page that contains a properly formatted table with the required data on the external JavaScript file. LibreJS visits this link and determines the version of jQuery linked from the original page is the one listed there, and flags it as free. All JavaScript is executed (and the title should turn green.)

Appendix D GNU Free Documentation License

Version 1.3, 3 November 2008

Copyright © 2000, 2001, 2002, 2007, 2008 Free Software Foundation, Inc. `http://fsf.org/`

Everyone is permitted to copy and distribute verbatim copies of this license document, but changing it is not allowed.

0. PREAMBLE

The purpose of this License is to make a manual, textbook, or other functional and useful document *free* in the sense of freedom: to assure everyone the effective freedom to copy and redistribute it, with or without modifying it, either commercially or non-commercially. Secondarily, this License preserves for the author and publisher a way to get credit for their work, while not being considered responsible for modifications made by others.

This License is a kind of "copyleft", which means that derivative works of the document must themselves be free in the same sense. It complements the GNU General Public License, which is a copyleft license designed for free software.

We have designed this License in order to use it for manuals for free software, because free software needs free documentation: a free program should come with manuals providing the same freedoms that the software does. But this License is not limited to software manuals; it can be used for any textual work, regardless of subject matter or whether it is published as a printed book. We recommend this License principally for works whose purpose is instruction or reference.

1. APPLICABILITY AND DEFINITIONS

This License applies to any manual or other work, in any medium, that contains a notice placed by the copyright holder saying it can be distributed under the terms of this License. Such a notice grants a world-wide, royalty-free license, unlimited in duration, to use that work under the conditions stated herein. The "Document", below, refers to any such manual or work. Any member of the public is a licensee, and is addressed as "you". You accept the license if you copy, modify or distribute the work in a way requiring permission under copyright law.

A "Modified Version" of the Document means any work containing the Document or a portion of it, either copied verbatim, or with modifications and/or translated into another language.

A "Secondary Section" is a named appendix or a front-matter section of the Document that deals exclusively with the relationship of the publishers or authors of the Document to the Document's overall subject (or to related matters) and contains nothing that could fall directly within that overall subject. (Thus, if the Document is in part a textbook of mathematics, a Secondary Section may not explain any mathematics.) The relationship could be a matter of historical connection with the subject or with related matters, or of legal, commercial, philosophical, ethical or political position regarding them.

The "Invariant Sections" are certain Secondary Sections whose titles are designated, as being those of Invariant Sections, in the notice that says that the Document is released under this License. If a section does not fit the above definition of Secondary then it is not allowed to be designated as Invariant. The Document may contain zero Invariant Sections. If the Document does not identify any Invariant Sections then there are none.

The "Cover Texts" are certain short passages of text that are listed, as Front-Cover Texts or Back-Cover Texts, in the notice that says that the Document is released under this License. A Front-Cover Text may be at most 5 words, and a Back-Cover Text may be at most 25 words.

A "Transparent" copy of the Document means a machine-readable copy, represented in a format whose specification is available to the general public, that is suitable for revising the document straightforwardly with generic text editors or (for images composed of pixels) generic paint programs or (for drawings) some widely available drawing editor, and that is suitable for input to text formatters or for automatic translation to a variety of formats suitable for input to text formatters. A copy made in an otherwise Transparent file format whose markup, or absence of markup, has been arranged to thwart or discourage subsequent modification by readers is not Transparent. An image format is not Transparent if used for any substantial amount of text. A copy that is not "Transparent" is called "Opaque".

Examples of suitable formats for Transparent copies include plain ASCII without markup, Texinfo input format, LaTeX input format, SGML or XML using a publicly available DTD, and standard-conforming simple HTML, PostScript or PDF designed for human modification. Examples of transparent image formats include PNG, XCF and JPG. Opaque formats include proprietary formats that can be read and edited only by proprietary word processors, SGML or XML for which the DTD and/or processing tools are not generally available, and the machine-generated HTML, PostScript or PDF produced by some word processors for output purposes only.

The "Title Page" means, for a printed book, the title page itself, plus such following pages as are needed to hold, legibly, the material this License requires to appear in the title page. For works in formats which do not have any title page as such, "Title Page" means the text near the most prominent appearance of the work's title, preceding the beginning of the body of the text.

The "publisher" means any person or entity that distributes copies of the Document to the public.

A section "Entitled XYZ" means a named subunit of the Document whose title either is precisely XYZ or contains XYZ in parentheses following text that translates XYZ in another language. (Here XYZ stands for a specific section name mentioned below, such as "Acknowledgements", "Dedications", "Endorsements", or "History".) To "Preserve the Title" of such a section when you modify the Document means that it remains a section "Entitled XYZ" according to this definition.

The Document may include Warranty Disclaimers next to the notice which states that this License applies to the Document. These Warranty Disclaimers are considered to be included by reference in this License, but only as regards disclaiming warranties: any other implication that these Warranty Disclaimers may have is void and has no effect on the meaning of this License.

2. VERBATIM COPYING

You may copy and distribute the Document in any medium, either commercially or noncommercially, provided that this License, the copyright notices, and the license notice saying this License applies to the Document are reproduced in all copies, and that you add no other conditions whatsoever to those of this License. You may not use technical measures to obstruct or control the reading or further copying of the copies you make or distribute. However, you may accept compensation in exchange for copies. If you distribute a large enough number of copies you must also follow the conditions in section 3.

You may also lend copies, under the same conditions stated above, and you may publicly display copies.

3. COPYING IN QUANTITY

If you publish printed copies (or copies in media that commonly have printed covers) of the Document, numbering more than 100, and the Document's license notice requires Cover Texts, you must enclose the copies in covers that carry, clearly and legibly, all these Cover Texts: Front-Cover Texts on the front cover, and Back-Cover Texts on the back cover. Both covers must also clearly and legibly identify you as the publisher of these copies. The front cover must present the full title with all words of the title equally prominent and visible. You may add other material on the covers in addition. Copying with changes limited to the covers, as long as they preserve the title of the Document and satisfy these conditions, can be treated as verbatim copying in other respects.

If the required texts for either cover are too voluminous to fit legibly, you should put the first ones listed (as many as fit reasonably) on the actual cover, and continue the rest onto adjacent pages.

If you publish or distribute Opaque copies of the Document numbering more than 100, you must either include a machine-readable Transparent copy along with each Opaque copy, or state in or with each Opaque copy a computer-network location from which the general network-using public has access to download using public-standard network protocols a complete Transparent copy of the Document, free of added material. If you use the latter option, you must take reasonably prudent steps, when you begin distribution of Opaque copies in quantity, to ensure that this Transparent copy will remain thus accessible at the stated location until at least one year after the last time you distribute an Opaque copy (directly or through your agents or retailers) of that edition to the public.

It is requested, but not required, that you contact the authors of the Document well before redistributing any large number of copies, to give them a chance to provide you with an updated version of the Document.

4. MODIFICATIONS

You may copy and distribute a Modified Version of the Document under the conditions of sections 2 and 3 above, provided that you release the Modified Version under precisely this License, with the Modified Version filling the role of the Document, thus licensing distribution and modification of the Modified Version to whoever possesses a copy of it. In addition, you must do these things in the Modified Version:

A. Use in the Title Page (and on the covers, if any) a title distinct from that of the Document, and from those of previous versions (which should, if there were any, be listed in the History section of the Document). You may use the same title as a previous version if the original publisher of that version gives permission.

B. List on the Title Page, as authors, one or more persons or entities responsible for authorship of the modifications in the Modified Version, together with at least five of the principal authors of the Document (all of its principal authors, if it has fewer than five), unless they release you from this requirement.

C. State on the Title page the name of the publisher of the Modified Version, as the publisher.

D. Preserve all the copyright notices of the Document.

E. Add an appropriate copyright notice for your modifications adjacent to the other copyright notices.

F. Include, immediately after the copyright notices, a license notice giving the public permission to use the Modified Version under the terms of this License, in the form shown in the Addendum below.

G. Preserve in that license notice the full lists of Invariant Sections and required Cover Texts given in the Document's license notice.

H. Include an unaltered copy of this License.

I. Preserve the section Entitled "History", Preserve its Title, and add to it an item stating at least the title, year, new authors, and publisher of the Modified Version as given on the Title Page. If there is no section Entitled "History" in the Document, create one stating the title, year, authors, and publisher of the Document as given on its Title Page, then add an item describing the Modified Version as stated in the previous sentence.

J. Preserve the network location, if any, given in the Document for public access to a Transparent copy of the Document, and likewise the network locations given in the Document for previous versions it was based on. These may be placed in the "History" section. You may omit a network location for a work that was published at least four years before the Document itself, or if the original publisher of the version it refers to gives permission.

K. For any section Entitled "Acknowledgements" or "Dedications", Preserve the Title of the section, and preserve in the section all the substance and tone of each of the contributor acknowledgements and/or dedications given therein.

L. Preserve all the Invariant Sections of the Document, unaltered in their text and in their titles. Section numbers or the equivalent are not considered part of the section titles.

M. Delete any section Entitled "Endorsements". Such a section may not be included in the Modified Version.

N. Do not retitle any existing section to be Entitled "Endorsements" or to conflict in title with any Invariant Section.

O. Preserve any Warranty Disclaimers.

If the Modified Version includes new front-matter sections or appendices that qualify as Secondary Sections and contain no material copied from the Document, you may at your option designate some or all of these sections as invariant. To do this, add their titles to the list of Invariant Sections in the Modified Version's license notice. These titles must be distinct from any other section titles.

You may add a section Entitled "Endorsements", provided it contains nothing but endorsements of your Modified Version by various parties—for example, statements of peer review or that the text has been approved by an organization as the authoritative definition of a standard.

You may add a passage of up to five words as a Front-Cover Text, and a passage of up to 25 words as a Back-Cover Text, to the end of the list of Cover Texts in the Modified Version. Only one passage of Front-Cover Text and one of Back-Cover Text may be added by (or through arrangements made by) any one entity. If the Document already includes a cover text for the same cover, previously added by you or by arrangement made by the same entity you are acting on behalf of, you may not add another; but you may replace the old one, on explicit permission from the previous publisher that added the old one.

The author(s) and publisher(s) of the Document do not by this License give permission to use their names for publicity for or to assert or imply endorsement of any Modified Version.

5. COMBINING DOCUMENTS

You may combine the Document with other documents released under this License, under the terms defined in section 4 above for modified versions, provided that you include in the combination all of the Invariant Sections of all of the original documents, unmodified, and list them all as Invariant Sections of your combined work in its license notice, and that you preserve all their Warranty Disclaimers.

The combined work need only contain one copy of this License, and multiple identical Invariant Sections may be replaced with a single copy. If there are multiple Invariant Sections with the same name but different contents, make the title of each such section unique by adding at the end of it, in parentheses, the name of the original author or publisher of that section if known, or else a unique number. Make the same adjustment to the section titles in the list of Invariant Sections in the license notice of the combined work.

In the combination, you must combine any sections Entitled "History" in the various original documents, forming one section Entitled "History"; likewise combine any sections Entitled "Acknowledgements", and any sections Entitled "Dedications". You must delete all sections Entitled "Endorsements."

6. COLLECTIONS OF DOCUMENTS

You may make a collection consisting of the Document and other documents released under this License, and replace the individual copies of this License in the various documents with a single copy that is included in the collection, provided that you follow the rules of this License for verbatim copying of each of the documents in all other respects.

You may extract a single document from such a collection, and distribute it individually under this License, provided you insert a copy of this License into the extracted document, and follow this License in all other respects regarding verbatim copying of that document.

7. AGGREGATION WITH INDEPENDENT WORKS

A compilation of the Document or its derivatives with other separate and independent documents or works, in or on a volume of a storage or distribution medium, is called an "aggregate" if the copyright resulting from the compilation is not used to limit the legal rights of the compilation's users beyond what the individual works permit. When the Document is included in an aggregate, this License does not apply to the other works in the aggregate which are not themselves derivative works of the Document.

If the Cover Text requirement of section 3 is applicable to these copies of the Document, then if the Document is less than one half of the entire aggregate, the Document's Cover Texts may be placed on covers that bracket the Document within the aggregate, or the electronic equivalent of covers if the Document is in electronic form. Otherwise they must appear on printed covers that bracket the whole aggregate.

8. TRANSLATION

Translation is considered a kind of modification, so you may distribute translations of the Document under the terms of section 4. Replacing Invariant Sections with translations requires special permission from their copyright holders, but you may include translations of some or all Invariant Sections in addition to the original versions of these Invariant Sections. You may include a translation of this License, and all the license notices in the Document, and any Warranty Disclaimers, provided that you also include the original English version of this License and the original versions of those notices and disclaimers. In case of a disagreement between the translation and the original version of this License or a notice or disclaimer, the original version will prevail.

If a section in the Document is Entitled "Acknowledgements", "Dedications", or "History", the requirement (section 4) to Preserve its Title (section 1) will typically require changing the actual title.

9. TERMINATION

You may not copy, modify, sublicense, or distribute the Document except as expressly provided under this License. Any attempt otherwise to copy, modify, sublicense, or distribute it is void, and will automatically terminate your rights under this License.

However, if you cease all violation of this License, then your license from a particular copyright holder is reinstated (a) provisionally, unless and until the copyright holder explicitly and finally terminates your license, and (b) permanently, if the copyright holder fails to notify you of the violation by some reasonable means prior to 60 days after the cessation.

Moreover, your license from a particular copyright holder is reinstated permanently if the copyright holder notifies you of the violation by some reasonable means, this is the first time you have received notice of violation of this License (for any work) from that copyright holder, and you cure the violation prior to 30 days after your receipt of the notice.

Termination of your rights under this section does not terminate the licenses of parties who have received copies or rights from you under this License. If your rights have been terminated and not permanently reinstated, receipt of a copy of some or all of the same material does not give you any rights to use it.

10. FUTURE REVISIONS OF THIS LICENSE

The Free Software Foundation may publish new, revised versions of the GNU Free Documentation License from time to time. Such new versions will be similar in spirit to the present version, but may differ in detail to address new problems or concerns. See http://www.gnu.org/copyleft/.

Each version of the License is given a distinguishing version number. If the Document specifies that a particular numbered version of this License "or any later version" applies to it, you have the option of following the terms and conditions either of that specified version or of any later version that has been published (not as a draft) by the Free Software Foundation. If the Document does not specify a version number of this License, you may choose any version ever published (not as a draft) by the Free Software Foundation. If the Document specifies that a proxy can decide which future versions of this License can be used, that proxy's public statement of acceptance of a version permanently authorizes you to choose that version for the Document.

11. RELICENSING

"Massive Multiauthor Collaboration Site" (or "MMC Site") means any World Wide Web server that publishes copyrightable works and also provides prominent facilities for anybody to edit those works. A public wiki that anybody can edit is an example of such a server. A "Massive Multiauthor Collaboration" (or "MMC") contained in the site means any set of copyrightable works thus published on the MMC site.

"CC-BY-SA" means the Creative Commons Attribution-Share Alike 3.0 license published by Creative Commons Corporation, a not-for-profit corporation with a principal place of business in San Francisco, California, as well as future copyleft versions of that license published by that same organization.

"Incorporate" means to publish or republish a Document, in whole or in part, as part of another Document.

An MMC is "eligible for relicensing" if it is licensed under this License, and if all works that were first published under this License somewhere other than this MMC, and subsequently incorporated in whole or in part into the MMC, (1) had no cover texts or invariant sections, and (2) were thus incorporated prior to November 1, 2008.

The operator of an MMC Site may republish an MMC contained in the site under CC-BY-SA on the same site at any time before August 1, 2009, provided the MMC is eligible for relicensing.

ADDENDUM: How to use this License for your documents

To use this License in a document you have written, include a copy of the License in the document and put the following copyright and license notices just after the title page:

```
Copyright (C)  year  your name.
Permission is granted to copy, distribute and/or modify this document
under the terms of the GNU Free Documentation License, Version 1.3
or any later version published by the Free Software Foundation;
with no Invariant Sections, no Front-Cover Texts, and no Back-Cover
Texts.  A copy of the license is included in the section entitled ''GNU
Free Documentation License''.
```

If you have Invariant Sections, Front-Cover Texts and Back-Cover Texts, replace the "with...Texts." line with this:

```
with the Invariant Sections being list their titles, with
the Front-Cover Texts being list, and with the Back-Cover Texts
being list.
```

If you have Invariant Sections without Cover Texts, or some other combination of the three, merge those two alternatives to suit the situation.

If your document contains nontrivial examples of program code, we recommend releasing these examples in parallel under your choice of free software license, such as the GNU General Public License, to permit their use in free software.

www.ingramcontent.com/pod-product-compliance
Lightning Source LLC
Chambersburg PA
CBHW060008230526
45472CB00008B/2000